C000163620

WHY ALL FISH* ARE BIASED

AND HOW TO TACKLE PREJUDICE

Lyndsey Oliver

*HUMANS

Published by Making MsChief®

MAKINGMsCHIEF
RESTORING BALANCE

For permission requests, email the author and publisher, at the address below.

Lyndsey Oliver

Chief@MakingMsChief.com

Making MsChief® Is a registered trading name of M4 Coaching Ltd.

Ordering Information:

For special orders, quantity sales and corporate sales, please email chief@makingmschief.com. Special discounts are available on quantity purchases by corporations, associations, and others. For details, contact the Chief MsChief Maker at the address above.

Why All Fish are Biased and How to Tackle Prejudice / Lyndsey Oliver. —1st ed.

ISBN 978-1-8381489-0-4

CONTENTS

For my gorgeous Minnows - Archie and Finlay.
You brighten up my world.
I love you.

*"The eye sees only what the mind is
prepared to comprehend."*

Robertson Davies

We all have biases. We all make judgements. We all experience stereotypes – you, me, and every human (a.k.a. Fish) on this planet.

No one is exempt (including me!). What is essential is that I know mine and you know yours, and we do not use these biases to oppress, marginalise, stereotype, and discriminate others.

Biases are cognitive shortcuts that allow us to instinctively categorise people (and things) without consciously thinking or being aware of it. Past experiences, mental, emotional, and psychological preconditioning are the basis for these cognitive shortcuts. Just like Newton's First Law of Motion, where an object will continue to move forward unless opposed by an unbalanced force, biases automatically guide our thinking unless we oppose them with change.

Biases are flaws in our thinking – they are generalisations based on beliefs and not facts. These beliefs (or cognitive shortcuts) are further compounded by our efforts to find evidence to support our hypotheses.

Unconscious biases are socially constructed stereotypes formed outside our conscious awareness.

The metaphor of the "Fish" and the "Fishbowl" is used to shift the narrative around bias. This book will support you on your journey towards effectively supporting and championing those marginalised in society.

This little book has a big goal: to liberate all Fish and create a world that is equal, equitable, and inclusive for all – and where people and planet live in balance with each other.

EQUALITY = SAMENESS

EQUALITY ASSUMES ALL FISH START FROM THE SAME BASE.

EQUITY = FAIRNESS

EQUITY ENSURES THAT ALL FISH GET ACCESS TO THE SAME OPPORTUNITIES.

THE FISH

"No one is born hating another person because of the colour of his skin, or his background, or his religion. People must learn to hate, and if they can learn to hate, they can be taught to love, for love comes more naturally to the human heart than its opposite."

Nelson Mandela

CHAPTER ONE

*"We are all born original – why is it so many
of us die copies?"*

Edward Young

A soul is born into the world. It can take many forms, but some are born into the world as Fish.

On the day it is born, the Fish has no concept of its appearance or the type of Fish it is. It has no idea if it is an ocean Fish, a river Fish, a sea Fish, or a Fishbowl Fish. It doesn't need to know.

The Fish is unique.

One of a kind.

It does not pretend to be something (or someone) other than who it is.

The Fish does not compare itself to anything or anyone else.

It is unapologetically itself.

It is who it is.

A Fish is born without bias.

As soon as they are born, the Fish are assigned labels – and "Fish" is the first. The initial label is typically closely followed by biological sex, gender, race, ethnicity, and name. Other Fish apply these labels – the baby Fish does not choose them. The cycle of socialisation has begun, and the Fish has no control over it.

Does the baby Fish even know that it is a Fish?

Does a Fish refer to itself as a Fish? I doubt it. The Fish just "is".

It is whole.

A soul (or maybe a sole) in a Fish suit.

CHAPTER TWO

BOXES AND LABELS

"I am who I am. Not who you think I am. Not who you want me to be. I am me."

Brigette Nicole

Who am I?
Who are you?
How can you answer the question without adding a label to the end of it?

I am.

"I am" ought to be enough of an explanation, but it isn't. "I am" is typically followed by so much more than a full stop.

As the Fish develops and grows, it forms an identity. The Fish is put into even more metaphorical boxes and given labels by which to define itself (or by which others define it).

The Fish begin to develop beliefs, stories, and narratives about who they are. These narratives differ from who they were on day one. Yet, the Fish believe that these new narratives are the truth – that these boxes and labels are who they are and who they have always been – yet they are not the truth.

The Fish are still who they are without the labels.

Time spent living in the Fishbowl with other Fish means that "I am" is often followed by labels, descriptors, and statements, rather than a full stop.

Labels are curious things. Some labels are:

- Assigned to the Fish at birth and last a lifetime.
- Assigned to the Fish at birth and are temporary.
- Assigned to the Fish at birth and are assumed to last a lifetime unless proven otherwise.
- Acquired as the Fish grows up.
- Facts.
- Lies.

Examples of boxes and labels that the Fish may acquire include:

- Name.
- Family name.
- Biological sex.
- Skin colour.
- Gender.
- Sexuality.
- Eye colour.
- Faith.
- Class.
- Able-bodied or disabled.

Examples of labels applied to the Fish at birth (and assumed to be facts until proven otherwise) include:

- Gender. The Fish is assumed male or female on the basis of the biological sex assigned at birth. Biological sex is not the same as gender (other Fish can get confused by this). When the Fish is born, the gender assigned to it at birth is typically male or female (and in some cases intersex), yet gender is non-binary. As the Fish grows up, it may realise that the gender assigned to it at birth is not its real (and innate) gender.

- Sexual identity. Typically, and traditionally, Baby Fish are raised as heterosexual. As the Fish grows up, it may realise that it is not (and never has been) a "heterosexual" Fish.

Boxes and labels are stereotypes and always come with a set of expectations and criteria to measure the Fish against. Stereotypes define how the Fish "should" be and how they "should" act.

"Shoulds" always belong to someone else and are projections or transferences by other Fish. "Shoulds" and "musts" are the basis of stereotypes.

Some fish take these "shoulds" on as their own. "Shoulds" keep the Fish small, scared, and fearful. The "shoulds" often become inner voices in the Fish's head.

11

Fish often find themselves twisting and contorting themselves to fit in and conform to these stereotypes, to meet the expectations of others.

These boxes and labels are not who they are, but who they are becoming.

As time goes by, the Fish moves further and further away from who it truly is.

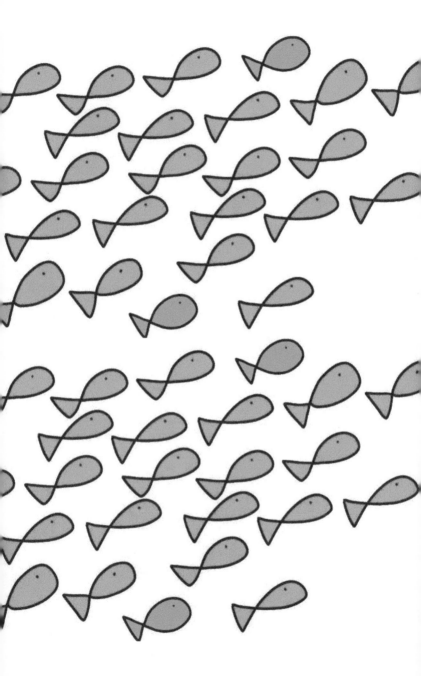

"Fitting in is about assessing a situation and becoming who you need to be, to be accepted. Belonging doesn't require us to change who we are. It requires us to be who we are."

Brené Brown

All Fish have a family of origin. Most Fish stay in that family unit while they are young, whereas others may move and grow up with a different family. It is inherent in the nature of a Fish to want to be part of the shoal. Fish want to feel a sense of belonging.

The unit that the Fish grows up in has a considerable influence on it. It is here that the Fish learns what it needs to do and how it must act to:

- Stay alive.
- Be safe.
- Feel loved.
- Belong.

The Fish learn that to feel a sense of belonging, they must act and behave in a certain way. Adaption is the price they pay for that sense of belonging, which also provides safety and security. Adaptation is the price they pay to be part of the shoal.

Conforming to these social rules results in the shoal (and the Fish) favouring "sameness" rather than "uniqueness". They quickly understand that it is essential to adapt, as their survival depends on it.

Fitting in requires conformity, shapeshifting, twisting, and contortion. This adaptation always leaves a feeling of incongruence within the Fish. There is a feeling that it is not enough to be who and what they are. This inner conflict is a consequence of adaptation.

The need to be someone or something different from who they truly are is another lie that the Fish have swallowed.

Fitting in is not the same as feeling a sense of belonging.

CHAPTER FOUR

A FISH'S SELF WORTH

"You determine your self-worth. You don't have to depend on someone telling you who you are."

Beyoncé

As the Fish grows up and takes on its labels, it can quickly forget who it was when it came into the Fishbowl on day one of its life.

The soul still exists in the Fish suit. Yet, it is no longer in the spotlight, shining brightly in all its wonder. The soul is pushed into the shadows influenced by labels and the need to conform.

The Fish may believe that their inherent value, worthiness, and ability to love and be loved has conditions attached.

The Fish learns to twist and contort itself to:

- Fit in.
- Be loved.
- Be liked.

- Be a "good" Fish.
- Please other Fish.

The consequence of this twisting, adaptation, and contortion is that the Fish becomes a duller, less vibrant version of itself, which has an impact on the Fish's inherent self-worth.

The truth is that the Fish's worthiness has no conditions. It was worthy the day it was born, and it is still worthy. Social conditioning feeds the Fish a lie, resulting in the Fish not believing this is so.

CHAPTER FIVE

MASKS AND ARMOUR

"You wear a mask for so long, you forget who you were beneath it."

Alan Moore

Twisting and contortion often result in the Fish putting on invisible masks and armour to protect itself in the Fishbowl.

The masks and armour are a defence.

The Fish wears their mask and armour for so long that they become invisible. The Fish believe that the mask and armour are part of who they are. The mask and armour can form part of the Fish's identity and can provide the Fish with a sense of safety and protection.

Masks and armour may be invisible to the Fish, yet it defines their existence – there is a heaviness, a weight, and a burden that the Fish endures as a consequence.

CHAPTER SIX

BECOMING AN "US" FISH

"The mind is everything. What you think you become."

Buddha

The Fish grows, learns, and develops in the Fishbowl. It shares its home Fishbowl with "Fish like us" or "Fish like me".

The Fish starts to become aware that there are "us" Fish and "them", or "other", Fish.

The "Fish like us" teach the Fish:

- What it means to be an "us" Fish.
- How to be a "Fish like us".
- The social systems and structures that exist within the Fishbowl, including:
    - The values, beliefs, rules, and laws to abide by.
    - The importance of power, authority, money, control, and religion.
    - Understanding who holds the power.

- The written and unwritten rules of what it means to be part of the shoal – how it needs to adapt to fit in.
- How to be a "good" Fish.
- The difference between a "good" Fish and a "bad" Fish.
- What the standard or "normal" Fish is, and whether they are classified as normal or not.
- About Fish that are "not like us" – the "them" Fish.

CHAPTER SEVEN

THE "THEM" FISH

*"Judging a Fish does not define who they are.
It defines who you are."*

F ish have many beliefs about Fish that are different from themselves. Beliefs are not facts, yet the Fish believe that they are facts, and they will have evidence to prove this. Fish like to be right.

The Fish starts to develop an "us versus them" mindset. Sometimes this is conscious; often, it is not.

An "us and them" mindset is a cultural and social construct based on binary thinking and rooted in fear, ignorance, confusion, and uncertainty. The Fish is socialised to learn:

- The differences between "us and them".
- To apply specific labels to the "them" Fish, or to put them in metaphorical boxes.
- To treat a Fish differently based on the labels that it has.

- That all Fish are not equal. This inequality is based on the boxes and labels applied to the Fish.
- Specific boxes and labels are socially more desirable than others (this is another lie the Fish have swallowed).

Binary thinking polarises the Fish into thinking that there are only two choices – us or them, me or you, this or that, black or white, right or wrong, good or bad, one or the other, etc.

Yet the Fishbowl is beautifully non-binary. Us *and* them, me *and* you, black *and* white, right *and* wrong, and a whole beautiful spectrum in between.

Binary thinking is divisive. The "us and them" mindset divides the Fish.

Binary thinking is another lie that the Fish have swallowed.

"Social constructs not only impact the art that is made, but they directly influence how art is presented and for whom it is preserved."

Julia Bullock

There is a standard Fish known as the "norm", which implies that all Fish without the "normal" label are the opposite of that – not normal.

The "normal" Fish are oblivious to the fact that they have this label and assume that the entire species of Fish experience the world in the same way. They are the standard which all Fish are measured against.

"Normal" is the most influential label that a Fish can have, as it gives the Fish power and privilege.

The "normal", or default Fish, tends to have several labels that make it "normal" or the "standard". Labels such as male, cisgender, heterosexual, heteronormative, educated, extroverted, masculine, neurotypical, able-bodied, and omnivore are just a few.

Normal is fictitious. There is no such thing as "normal". It is a social construct created by the "normal" group to maintain power, status, wealth, and control.

The Fish have swallowed another lie, which is absorbed into their being.

In 2015 there were more Fish called John (Dory) leading FTSE 100 companies than women.

CHAPTER NINE

THE PRIVILEGED FEW

"To be white, or straight, or male or middle class is to be simultaneously ubiquitous and invisible. You're everywhere you look, and you're the standard against which everyone else is measured. You're like water, like air. People will tell you they went to see a 'woman doctor' or they will say they went to see 'the doctor.' People will tell you they have a 'gay colleague' or they'll tell you about a colleague. A white person will be happy to tell you about a 'Black friend,' but when that same person simply mentions a 'friend,' everyone will assume the person is white. Any college course that doesn't have the word 'woman' or 'gay' or 'minority' in its title is a course about men, heterosexuals, and white people. But we call those courses 'literature,' 'history' or 'political science'. This invisibility is political."

Michael S. Kimmel

The normal Fish have privilege.

Privilege is an unfair advantage based on the labels that a fish has. It is a system of oppression set up to serve the "normal" Fish and detrimentally impact all other Fish. Privilege does not create an equal playing field.

Many Fish reject the idea that their labels bestow a privilege upon them. They argue that privilege is only experienced by those who live in the castles or serve in powerful roles.

It is not true.

To say that someone has privilege is not to deny those with privilege have not suffered or had hard lives, or that they have experienced trauma in the Fishbowl. Many have. This misunderstanding is often why some Fish find it hard to accept that they have privilege, or that they knowingly take advantage of it.

Privilege is often unconscious.

Privileged Fish swim in the Fishbowl unhindered, assisted, and advantaged by the current. They also have access to tools and resources that accelerate them through the Fishbowl. There are no blockages for them to navigate, they swim with the flow, and their path to their chosen destination is rarely impeded. Yes, they are still "working", as it takes effort to swim, but they can quickly and easily navigate their way around the Fishbowl. They can access all areas (at any time) without being impeded or fearing for their safety. Nobody stops them or asks them why they are in a specific area – unless another Fish asks for directions.

Privileged Fish rarely look over their fins to check their safety, and they have greater access to jobs, loans, education, housing, and healthcare. Any rules and legislation serve to their advantage, and if they break the laws, the consequences are more lenient than if the "other" Fish were to do the same thing.

The system of privilege means that "other" marginalised Fish (also known as minority groups) always swim against the current. The more minority labels a Fish has, the more blockages impede its path and the greater the effect on the Fish. Minority labels disadvantage the Fish and make it harder for the Fish to progress and navigate its way around the Fishbowl.

The "other" Fish often find that they can't access certain areas. They are regularly stopped (by Fish with more authority) and pulled over to the side of the Fishbowl to ask why they are in certain areas and what they are doing. They continually face doubt and suspicion as they navigate their way past the boulders, weeds, locks, weirs, and whirlpools in their path.

The privileged Fish do not see all of the hurdles that the "other" Fish have to overcome. Many believe that the minority Fish are making their troubles up, or exaggerating, and some will even argue that they have brought their troubles on themselves because of their attitude. Some Fish think that the "other" Fish are not as smart (another lie they have swallowed).

Many privileged Fish refuse to acknowledge that an oppressive system exists, especially those that have faced trauma, hard times, and struggle in their lives.

This lack of acknowledgement and refusal to change their beliefs (and the system) means that the cycle of oppression continues.

THE FISHBOWL

"Earth provides enough to satisfy every man's needs, but not every man's greed."

Mahatma Gandhi

"Human use, population and technology have reached that certain stage where Mother Earth no longer accepts our presence with silence."

Dalai Lama

CHAPTER TEN

A FISHBOWL CALLED HOME

"Fish did not discover water. In fact because they are completely immersed in it they live unaware of its existence. Similarly, when a conduct is normalised by a dominant cultural environment it becomes invisible."

Marshall McLuhan

The Fishbowl is the Fish's home. Fishbowls come in all shapes and sizes. A Fishbowl might be as small as a plastic bag (usually found in a fairground) or as vast as the ocean.

Rivers. Ponds. Lakes and seas – these are all Fishbowls.

The Fish grows and develops within the Fishbowl. It is here the Fish learns the rules of behaviour and "how to be a Fish". Its development, attitudes, behaviours, values, and beliefs are influenced by the water and the Fish that it is surrounded by.

The Fish does not necessarily know or have an awareness that it is living in a Fishbowl because it is all that the Fish knows.

CHAPTER ELEVEN

A FISHBOWL HIERARCHY

"Tug on anything in nature, and you will find it connected to everything else."

John Muir

ll Fishbowls exist within a hierarchy. All Fishbowls are interconnected, yet many Fish don't like to believe that this is so. Some Fish even refuse to believe that the Fishbowl is not round.

There is a Fishbowl that sits at the top of the hierarchy and dominates all others. Those with most privilege swim and live in the Fishbowl at the top. Those at the top have the most privilege, status, power, and control and determine the dominant culture.

The dominant culture teaches all Fish how to play their role in the system of oppression. "Good" behaviour and conformity is rewarded, whereas "bad" behaviour is punished. The definition of "good" and "bad" is dictated by the "norm" Fish. "Other" Fish generally face more significant consequences, punishment, and penalties for conduct that goes against societal norms.

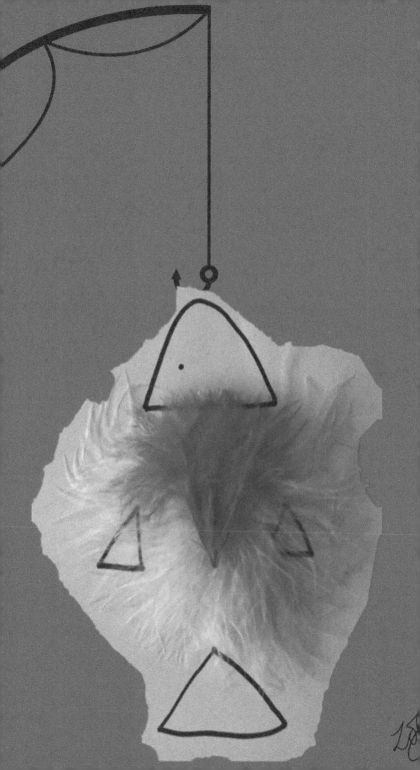

"Even small Fish are Fish."

Czech Proverb

Where Fish are different from the norm, there are mechanisms used (some subtle and unconscious and others not so much) by the most privileged Fish to dominate and control them.

The privileged Fish rule using fear and portraying the "other" Fish as dangerous or bad. There are numerous ways to achieve this, including the use of invalidating language (if applied to humans, we would call this dehumanisation) by referring to the "other" Fish as "aliens" or "savages". They can also objectify the other Fish, for example saying, "look at the pair of fins on that".

Invalidation and objectification result in the "other" Fish being seen as "non-Fish". This technique disconnects the Fish from their hearts and reinforces the myth that it is not safe to be different.

Those Fish labelled as "other" are often physically, mentally, emotionally, and psychologically harmed because of their labels. They may experience bias, discrimination, marginalisation, and oppression – and in some cases are murdered because of the labels that they have.

The "us" Fish and the "them" Fish can share the same Fishbowl, or they may exist in different Fishbowls. There is usually a set of explicit and implicit rules that apply to the "other" Fish. There may be both visible and invisible barriers that divide the Fish.

If the Fishbowl has a castle, then only the most privileged Fish will live in it.

The privileged Fish want to control and dominate the "other" Fish. They have many tools (and weapons) for doing so, including legislation, incarceration, gaslighting, stereotyping, silencing, restricting movement, deanimalisation, objectification, lack of access to money, Fishbowls, education, and jobs, and in the worst possible scenario, murder and genocide.

The system is not fair and causes harm.

The system needs to change.

The right to control is just an illusion.

"Freedom of movement is the very essence of our free society – once the right to travel is curtailed, all other rights suffer."

William O. Douglas

O nly the most privileged Fish can swim and move between the Fishbowls (if they choose to do so). Freedom of movement decreases the lower down on the hierarchy a Fish exists. Privilege gives access. It provides a passport.

Some Fish will only ever swim in their home Fishbowl, never venturing beyond the limits of their home. This could be by choice, or it may be due to the hierarchical rules defined above.

Many Fish are not allowed in certain Fishbowls. These Fishbowls may be further off-limits, as Fish often build barriers and walls to keep other Fish out. Fish that are "not like" them.

There are some Fishbowls that let the other Fish in – but only after they have navigated their way through a seemingly impossible obstacle course. The "other" Fish have to work at least twice as hard to gain access to these Fishbowls.

The privileged Fish also create stories about some of the other Fishbowls and how these are "dangerous" or "ghettos", which drives the belief that "other" Fish are dangerous. This results in further stereotyping, bias, oppression, and deanimalisation of the Fish that live in these Fishbowls. The truth is that these Fish are not dangerous – the "danger" is in the narratives and lies that the Fish swallow as truth.

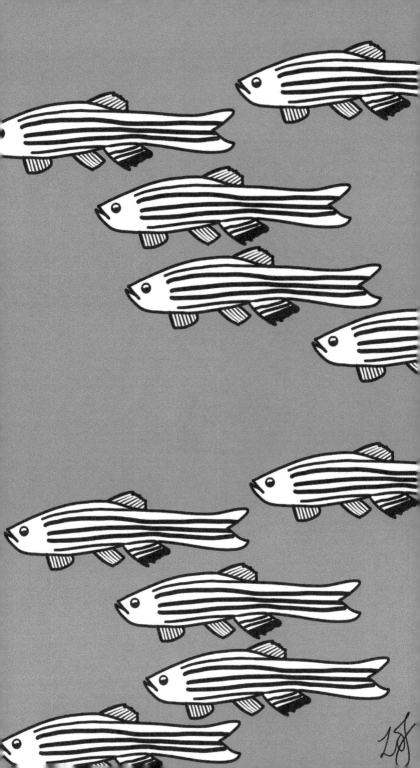

CHAPTER FOURTEEN

CONGREGATIONAL FISHBOWLS

"I think fitting in is highly overrated. I'd rather just fit out. Fitting out means being who you are, even when people insist that you have to change. Fitting out means taking up space, not apologising for yourself, and not agreeing with those who seek to label you with stereotypes."

Golda Poretsky

There are "home" Fishbowls that the Fish live in and "congregational" Fishbowls, which are visited for specific reasons. For example, Fish may gather in these bowls to:

- Be educated.
- Work.
- Practice their faith or religion.
- Exercise.

Congregational Fishbowls differ in size, shape, and culture, and these differences further shape and influence the views and beliefs of the Fish that exist within the congregational community.

The cultures of congregational Fishbowls are significantly affected by the "founding Fish", as they:

- Chose the bowl.
- Created the original culture.
- Chose the first Fish to join them.
- Choose who is allowed in.

Congregational Fishbowls also have a hierarchical structure, and those that swim at the top generally have more privilege, status, and power.

Those that congregate in these bowls can be a mix of the present-day Fish, as well as the invisible fin-ger-print from Fish that have come before, yet still have an influence on the culture in the form of stories, symbols, rituals, routines, systems, power structures, beliefs, and values.

Within the congregational Fishbowl precedence is given to the type of Fish that will "fit in" with the culture. Consciously and unconsciously, there is often a preference to recruit "Fish like us". Those Fish that are different from the "congregational norm" will often develop mechanisms to fit in.

Some of these congregational Fishbowls will paint themselves as diverse and inclusive (and they like to think that they are) and that all Fish are welcome. They "talk the talk" on diversity and inclusion. But the reality of representation will always show how diverse and inclusive a Fishbowl truly is. If a congregational Fishbowl says that they are diverse and inclusive, yet 99% of the population is a specific colour or gender or have a particular type of fin, then reality speaks for itself.

CHAPTER FIFTEEN

THE DELUSION OF INCLUSION

"Stand for something or you will fall for anything. Today's mighty oak is yesterday's nut that held its ground."

Rosa Parks

Many of the privileged Fish mistakenly believe that the "other" Fish are treated equally and equitably and that "all Fish are the same". Many think that if there is an inequity, it has nothing to do with the labels that the "other" Fish have – it's a consequence of their behaviour and actions. It's their fault.

This is not correct. It is bullshit.

It's another lie that the Fish have swallowed.

The interconnected nature of the Fishbowl and the effects of the water (and the bias of the Fish) result in a lack of inclusion. Real inclusion requires the collapse of the hierarchy, barriers to be dismantled, walls to be demolished, and all Fish enabled to be free to move, without hindrance, swimming with the current and not against it.

THE FISH USED TO
SEGREGATE FISH WITH
CERTAIN LABELS.

HILST SEGREGATION IS NO
ONGER PRACTISED, EXCLUSION
TILL OCCURS AND YET MANY
SH ARE BLIND TO IT.

INTEGRATION IS OFTEN MISTAKE
FOR INCLUSION.

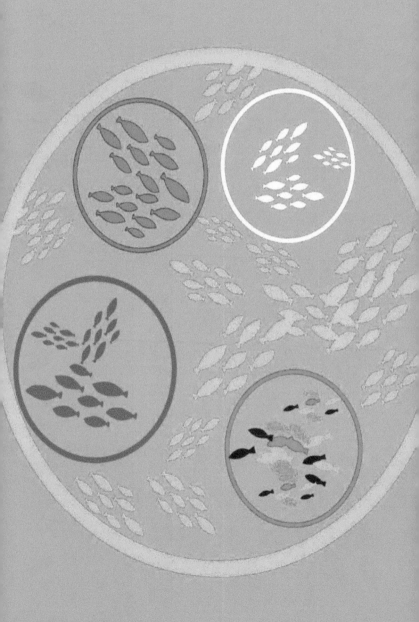

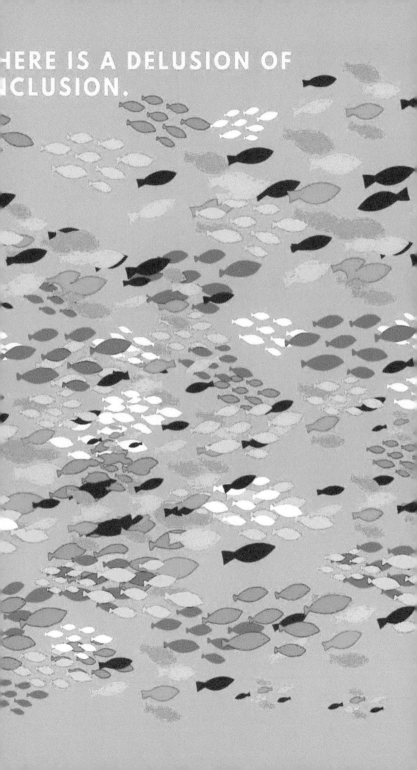

HERE IS A DELUSION OF
INCLUSION.

THE WATER

"Water is the driving force of all nature."

Leonardo Da Vinci

CHAPTER SIXTEEN

A FUNDAMENTAL NEED

"A Fish has no concept of water."

Janet Fitch

All Fish swim in the water.

A Fish may not be aware of the water because it is everywhere – it surrounds the Fish. Water existed long before the Fish.

Water is similar to the air that humans breathe. Humans don't see it, but it exists, and without it, they would die.

The Fish doesn't know any different – water is water.

Water is the culture, and it carries within it the systems and processes of socialisation.

THE CYCLE OF SOCIALISATION

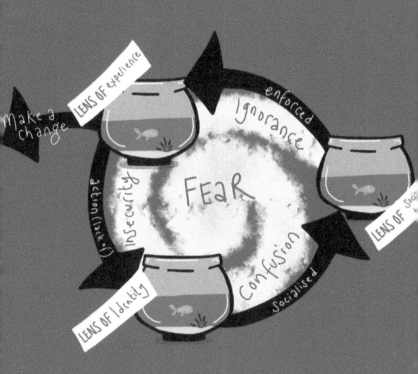

ADAPTED FROM HARRO, B (2000). THE CYCLE OF SOCIALISATION.
READINGS FOR DIVERSITY AND SOCIAL JUSTICE.

CHAPTER SEVENTEEN

"If you're always trying to be normal, you will never know how amazing you can be."

Maya Angelou

The cycle of socialisation teaches the Fish how to play roles in oppression and how to respect the systems that shape the Fish's thinking, being, and acting in the Fishbowl. When faced with having to acknowledge the system of oppression, the Fish often blame uncontrollable forces, other Fish, or themselves, as opposed to the system.

The cycle is fuelled and enabled by a culture of fear, ignorance, confusion, and uncertainty. The system becomes self-fulfilling and leads to a state of unconsciousness in the Fish (regarding the oppressive system), which often continues until there is a specific event, or set of events, that liberates the Fish from that thinking.

Lens of Identity

The Fish is born into the Home Fishbowl with no guilt, no consciousness of oppression, and with specific mechanics in place.

Socialisation in the Home Fishbowl is taught on a personal level by family and other Fish that are loved and trusted. These Fish are the shapers of expectations, norms, values, roles, and rules. It is then provided with limited information, or misinformation and where it begins to learn about stereotypes, biases, prejudices, history, and tradition.

Lens of Socialisation and Teaching

In the congregational Fishbowls, and as the Fish grows up, it is bombarded with messages from institutions (churches, schools, television, legal systems, medicine, business) and culture (song lyrics, art, language, media, patterns of thought) on both a conscious and unconscious level. This instils ideas, beliefs, and behaviours.

These are further enforced and stigmatised through:
- Systemic rewards and punishments.
- Privilege and persecution.
- Discrimination and empowerment.

Lens of Experience

These motivations can result in dissonance, silence, anger, invalidation, collusion, guilt, self-hatred, violence, and the internalisation of patterns of power.

The cycle perpetuates itself and leads to a state of unconsciousness in the Fish (regarding systems of oppression). The Fish avoids any action that could create waves in the Fishbowl to ensure that the status quo is maintained.

CHAPTER EIGHTEEN

"How is it possible that the most intellectual creature to ever walk planet Earth is destroying its only home."

Jane Goodall

The water at the top of the hierarchical Fishbowl is the cleanest, as it has more access to sunlight and fewer weeds.

All Fish are shitting in the water and not cleaning it up.

Shit sinks.

Shit stinks.

The further down the hierarchy a Fish's "home" in the Fishbowl, the dirtier the water.

The Fish at the top tend to ignore the problem (because they can't see it) and often blame the "other" Fish lower down in the Fishbowl. It's a tactic of those with privilege to point their fin(ger) at others.

All Fish shit – it's a natural process. Shitting in the water would not necessarily be a problem, as there are weeds that naturally occur in the Fishbowl, which act as a natural filtering system to keep the water clean. The issue is that some of the more privileged Fish are removing the weeds from the Fishbowl to make money, which further adds to the issue.

The shit infiltrates all systems within the home and congregational Fishbowls. The Fish are in effect eating their shit, which has a detrimental impact on the water and the Fish.

The Fish are complicit in the destruction of the ecosystem because the Fish value money and power more than the weeds.

CHAPTER NINETEEN

THE WATER IS POLLUTED

"Only when the last tree has died, and the last river has been poisoned and the last Fish been caught will we realise that we can not eat money."

Cree Indian Proverb

The water in the Fishbowl is polluted (even at the top of the bowl) and toxic. It is insidious.

Not only do the Fish shit in the bowl, but they also discard their rubbish. It too sinks.

Other elements cause pollution, including historical events, politics, education, media, marketing, news, fake news, advertising, books, music, film, art, narratives, legislation, and much more.

Philosophical pollutants include toxic beliefs, lies, the worshipping of money, materialism, status, and power.

Three groups of Fish respond to this issue:

The Maintainers

Fish that know the water is toxic, yet they see the privileged and powerful Fish ruling the Fishbowl and feel powerless to make a change. So the norm is maintained.

The Deniers

Fish that deny pollution exists and has an impact on the Fish, the water, or the bowl. They are oblivious and numb to the toxicity.

The Do-ers

Fish that know there is an issue and are actively trying to change it. These are the change-makers, activists, and rebel Fish. They seek new solutions for the Fish, the water, and the Fishbowl. The powerful Fish (and media) often portray these Fish as troublemakers. They are not. The troublemakers are the Privileged Fish that are fuelling the toxic cycle (and getting away with It).

CHAPTER TWENTY

WATER AFFECTS FISH

"The most common way people give up their power is by thinking they don't have any."

Alice Walker

Fish swim in the water, and the water is toxic. The Fish are not impervious, and so inevitably the Fish absorb that toxicity.

The Fish absorb the toxins and pollutants into their bodies and their minds through their skin and gills. The water is taken in through the mouth and forced out through the gill passages, and the dissolved oxygen then moves into the bloodstream and travels into the Fish's cells. The water infiltrates and impacts every single part of its being.

The quality of the water has a deep and profound impact on the Fish and influences its development – mentally, physically, emotionally, and spiritually.

The longer the exposure to the pollutants, the harder it will be to detoxify the mind and body of the Fish. Many believe that Fish cannot change. They can – if the Fish choose to do so.

Some Fish in the bowl are toxic to their core. They spew their toxicity out into the water, and towards the "other" Fish, which further adds to the pollution and the negative culture in the Fishbowl. They are consciously divisive, and their perspectives are extreme. Their hatred of the "other" is blatant. They believe that Fish "like them" are superior to all other Fish. It can seem as if these Fish are impenetrable, yet the toxicity of the water, and their own, is killing them.

The water is toxic.

The Fish are toxic.

The Fishbowl is toxic.

THE UNFORTUNATE TRUTH

"No one wants the truth if it is inconvenient."

Arthur Miller

CHAPTER TWENTY-ONE

ALL FISH ARE BIASED

"Most white people are more worried about being called racist than about whether or not their actions are in fact racist or harmful."

Austin Channing Brown

All Fish are biased whether they are conscious of it or not – this includes the so-called "good Fish".

Most Fish don't think of themselves as being discriminatory and having biases, yet some of their daily actions unintentionally perpetuate systems of oppression.

Denying the existence of biases and not recognising them ensures that the discrimination, oppression, division, separation, and exclusion of the "other" Fish continue.

CHAPTER TWENTY-TWO

BOXES AND LABELS ARE SOCIAL CONSTRUCTS

"Definitions belong to the definers, not the defined."

Toni Morrison

Every Fish is unique.

The division and separation of Fish by their labels, or grouping them into specific boxes, is a social construct set up to serve the privileged few.

The system socialises the Fish to play specific roles, which is underpinned by a power dynamic, fuelled by fear, ignorance, confusion, and insecurity.

These social constructs are further lies that the Fish have swallowed.

Lies add to the toxicity of the water and the Fish.

CHAPTER TWENTY-THREE

THE DANGER OF A GOOD FISH

"The opposite of racist isn't "not racist." It is "anti-racist." What's the difference? One endorses either the idea of a racial hierarchy as a racist, or racial equality as an anti-racist. One either believes problems are rooted in groups of people, as a racist, or locates the roots of problems in power and policies, as an anti-racist. One either allows racial inequities to persevere, as a racist, or confronts racial inequities, as an anti-racist. There is no in-between safe space of 'not racist."

Ibram X. Kendi

ood Fish like to think that they are immune to the toxicity. They refuse to accept the fact that they could be toxic – which is like denying that a Fish has a shadow.

Toxicity is often associated with being a "bad" Fish, and they are a "good" Fish. "Good" Fish are fervently attached to the belief that good Fishes can't be toxic. And they do not want to be labelled as an x-ist, or a y-ist, or, or, or. Often what these Fish may say is that:

- We are all Fish.
- All Fish lives matter.
- I don't see difference.
- All Fish are the same.

They might justify their goodness by saying that they "have friends that are "other" Fish, or they are married to an "other" fish (the fact that "other" Fish are parts of their lives seems to make them think that they are immune to the toxicity).

Denial and the Fish's defensive behaviour blocks curiosity, connection, and the ability to truly listen and empathise with the experiences of "other" Fish. The "good" Fish causes harm to the "other", which paradoxically is what they are not trying to do.

If the "good" Fish cause harm, then their discomfort can result in many defensive responses, including centring themselves and blaming the "other" Fish rather than admitting that their actions were harmful.

The Fish's attachment to being a "good" Fish is dangerous as they are blind and unwilling to face how their privilege, biases, beliefs, values, and behaviour maintain the system of oppression rather than dismantling it.

The "good" Fish, due to their fragility and attachment to identity, continue to enable the oppressive system to persist. It is self-perpetuating.

A "good" Fish can still do bad things.

"Good" Fish also have unconscious biases – it doesn't make them "bad".

CHAPTER TWENTY-FOUR

THE WATER WILL CONTINUE TO SUSTAIN LIFE, BUT NOT NECESSARILY THE LIFE OF THE FISH

"If a frog is put suddenly into boiling water, it will jump out, but if the frog is put in tepid water which is then brought to a boil slowly, it will not perceive the danger and will be cooked to death."

Anon

The Fish need the Fishbowl, yet the Fishbowl does not need the Fish.

The Fish have forgotten this. It is collective amnesia, yet at their core, all Fish know this as a truth.

For the Fish to survive, the water needs to be balanced. The environment needs to be within a specific temperature range and to contain the right food and nutrients. If the water becomes too toxic or the temperature levels move outside of those ranges, there is a risk that Fish may die.

The Fish are dependent on the water and the Fishbowl for their survival.

The Fishbowl and the water are not dependent on the Fish.

The culture that the Fish create and the toxins that are released produce an effect that heats the water. If the Fish continue to heat the water, they will be boiled like the frog.

CHAPTER TWENTY-FIVE

THE FISH ARE BEING IMPACTED

"The trouble is you think you have time."

Buddha

The Fish are already adversely impacted by the toxicity of the water.

The pollutants and toxins are causing:

Viruses to spread amongst the Fish population, which cause sickness and death.

Food supplies to diminish, which results in competition for food.

A rise in the water temperature, which impacts many things, including the health of the Fish, the supply of food, and a reduction in habitable space, as some parts of the Fishbowl are hotter than others.

The Fish to migrate to other parts of the Fishbowl when their part becomes uninhabitable, which causes further tensions and has a heating effect on the water.

Fish to feel angry at the lack of inclusion and equality. When conflict arises, it results in the temperature of the water rising further.

The Fish to adapt to "fit in". Adaptation adds to the toxicity of the Fish and the water.

Conflict between certain parts of the Fishbowl, which decimate specific populations of Fish and cause millions of Fish to seek refuge in other parts of the Fishbowl. This again causes tensions between the Fish and further heats the water.

The water to heat and evaporate, which further toxifies the remaining water and reduces the habitable space for the Fish.

A culture of competition that drives a destructive "win at all cost" and "be number one" mentality between the Fish. Again, this further heats the water.

The Fish to develop a blame culture of fin-ger pointing and a lack of accountability. Again, this has a heating effect on the water.

Fish to feel powerless and lack accountability for making change. Powerlessness has a heating effect on the water.

The current dynamic in the Fishbowl is not sustainable. If the pollution continues and radical changes do not occur, the Fishbowl will become uninhabitable, and the Fish will die.

The uncomfortable truth is that the Fish are already dying.

THE SOLUTION

"The master's tools will never dismantle the master's house. They may allow us to temporarily beat him at his own game, but they will never allow us to bring about genuine change."

Audre Lorde

CHAPTER TWENTY-SIX

MAKE THE UNCONSCIOUS CONSCIOUS

*"Until you make the unconscious conscious,
it will direct your life, and you
will call it fate."*

Carl Jung

Only 5–10% of a Fish's thoughts, values, beliefs, and behaviours are conscious. The remaining 90–95% are unconscious. This limits the cognitive understanding of the Fish. Unless the unconscious is made conscious, the unconscious mind (and fear) drives the show.

For a Fish to identify, understand, and overcome the effect of its biases, it is essential to work with both the conscious and the unconscious. Otherwise, the systems of oppression will continue and the water will continue to heat and become more toxic.

When a Fish makes its unconscious conscious and dismantles its biases, it is then able to make conscious choices and then can choose to act in a manner that is inclusive.

When this happens, it reduces the toxicity in the Fish and the water and has a cooling effect on the temperature of the water.

CHAPTER TWENTY-SEVEN

DISMANTLE

"After a lifetime of embodying difference, I have no desire to be equal. I want to deconstruct the structural power of a system that marked me out as different. I don't wish to be assimilated into the status quo. I want to be liberated from all negative assumptions that my characteristics bring."

Reni Eddo-Lodge

There is a belief amongst the Fish that Fish can't change who they are.

Yes, they can't change the colour of their fins, or the colour of their eyes. There are a few things that are fixed. Yet, they can change a lot more than they think.

Fish can change identities, beliefs, values, behaviours, and mindsets. They can learn new skills and capabilities. They can make their biases conscious and change them so that they can be inclusive. They have the ability and the power to dismantle the systems of oppression that exist in the Fishbowl.

Dismantling starts with the Fish. As individual Fish dismantle their own biases, it has a direct effect on and weakens the system of oppression.

The walls and barriers the Fish have built up within themselves need to be collapsed. In doing so, it collapses part of the system too. This is the universal law of cause and effect in action.

While dismantling their own biases, it is essential that the Fish also advocate to dismantle:

- The walls and barriers that restrict freedom of movement between parts of the Fishbowl.
- All systems of oppression.
- The power structures set up to benefit and serve those with privilege.
- Collective biases, stereotypes, prejudices, values, and beliefs that divide rather than unite.
- Processes and systems that support systems of oppression.

CHAPTER TWENTY-EIGHT

DETOXIFY AND DECONSTRUCT

"If you can imagine it, you can achieve it. If you can dream it, you can become it."

Arthur William Ward

A shift is required. The Fish need to detoxify, deconstruct, and disentangle to create a new reality:

Detoxify:

The water.

- Remove the pollutants to restore balance and equilibrium.
- Infuse the water with love and respect towards others.
- Actively plant, support and protect the weeds, which are the natural filtering system of the Fishbowl.

The Fish.

- Start with increasing self-awareness.

- Operate from a place of love and positive intent – this has a neutralising effect on the Fish and the water.
- Focus on collaboration rather than competition.

Deconstruct:

- Identities, thoughts, beliefs, values, and behaviours that lead to division, stereotyping, bias, marginalisation, and oppression.
- The pattern, processes, systems and structures that place profit above the health and welfare of the Fish, the water, and the Fishbowl.
- Systems and processes that support oppression.
- Hierarchy by removing leaders and those at the top of the Fishbowl that reinforce the status quo.

The aim of detoxification and deconstruction is to:

- Restore balance within the Fishbowl.
- Create a culture and ecosystem that is balanced between the Fish, the water, and the Fishbowl.
- Ensure mutual respect and a symbiotic relationship.
- Build a circular economy centred in sustainability.
- Create policies, processes, systems, and legislation rooted in inclusion, equality, equity, and respect for all Fishes *and* the environment.
- Celebrate each and every Fish for its individuality and uniqueness and the value their difference brings to the collective.

- Enable freedom of movement and equal access to resources for all Fish, regardless of their labels.
- Allow all Fish to feel a true sense of togetherness and interdependence.

CHAPTER TWENTY-NINE

THE ALCHEMY OF INCLUSION

"It takes a huge effort to free yourself from memory."

Paolo Coelho

Inclusion is transformative.

Inclusion is the balance between yin and yang. It is restorative.

Inclusion is the acceptance of all that is.

Inclusion alchemises toxicity and transforms it into an environment that enables all Fish to thrive.

Alchemy means the Fish detaching themselves from some of their inherited stories and leaving those stories in the past to make room for, and create, a new narrative.

Alchemy moves the Fish from awareness to accountability, from fear to curiosity, from lack to abundance.

Alchemy results in an expansion of space and has a cooling effect on the Fish and the Water.

CHAPTER THIRTY

TOGETHERNESS

"When "I" is replaced with "we", even illness becomes wellness."

Malcolm X

nclusion often talks about "belonging", yet what the Fish need is togetherness.

Fish don't belong to anyone or anything. Belonging has an element of "possession", and Fish are not possessions to be owned.

Togetherness is the energy of interdependence – that "we all need each other and can work and live together, equally, equitably, and inclusively".

You are free. I am free. Together we are free.

ALLY

is a verb, not a noun.

CHAPTER THIRTY-ONE

ALLYSHIP

"Allyship is not an identity but a practice."

Layla F Saad

At the core of inclusion is allyship. "Ally" is a verb, not a noun. It is:

- Proactive.
- A journey, not a destination.
- Transformative and not performative.
- Talking the talk and walking the walk.
- An equal balance of learning and unlearning.
- Being accountable for your education and actions – every single day.
- Listening more than talking.
- The ability to be open-minded and open-hearted.

To practice Allyship, the Fish must:

- Unpack the lies and the mistruths they have swallowed.

- Make their unconscious conscious.
- Know that they will fuck up. Own the mistake, learn from it, own the impact, and commit to doing better.
- Know their biases and combat them.
- Watch their language, as language can be divisive.
- Understand their privilege and transfer the benefits.
- Adopt an intersectional approach.
- Identify where there is bias in policies and systems and change them.
- Provide support for other Fish (what the other Fish need versus what the privileged Fish think that they need).
- Speak up – silence is complicity.
- Have the messy conversations – the conversations that matter.
- Raise and amplify the voices of the "other" Fish. Turn over the mic and step out of the spotlight.
- Build safe spaces for the community.
- Stand up. Stand in solidarity. Advocate.
- Actively participate in social justice movements.
- Act. Actions speak louder than words.
- Vote.

A note to the privileged Fish.

It is more important to practice being an effective ally rather than trying to be a "good" ally.

Know that you will mess up. You won't get it right all of the time – own your mistakes – there is magic in the messiness.

And remember, it's not about you. Don't expect a gold medal for your efforts.

THE CYCLE OF LIBERATION

CHAPTER THIRTY-TWO

LIBERATION

"My liberty depends on you being free too."

Barack Obama

L iberation is defined as "an occasion when something or someone is released or made free. Referring to activities connected with removing the disadvantages experienced by particular groups within society".

There is a cyclical process common to many social change efforts known as the Cycle of Liberation.

A set of qualities exists at the core of the cycle which operate at an individual and collective level. These qualities strengthen with each Fish connection. Liberation for the Fish is:

- The practice of self-love and learning to love all others, regardless of differences.
- Finding balance individually and collectively.
- Taking charge of their destiny and creating a world that the Fish want to live in.

- The ability to make change happen and a belief that they can succeed.
- Joy at their collective efficacy and their ability to survive in the Fishbowl.
- The knowledge that the Fish are not alone.
- Being led by their hearts, minds, and gut instinct.
- Relentless commitment to the goal of equity, justice, and love.
- Knowing that liberation is far more significant than a single Fish – that Fish are connected to all living beings.
- Commitment to envisioning and creating a better, more balanced Fishbowl.

There is no specific start or endpoint to this process, which is why Allyship is a journey and a practice – not an identity.

For liberation to be achieved, change is required at three levels:

- Inter – within the Fish.
- Intra – between the Fish.
- Systemic – within the system.

Waking Up

This stage marks the beginning of the Cycle of Liberation and is an intrapersonal change. As a result of a critical awakening or the result of a slow shift in the Fish's perspective and worldview, it is here the Fish may begin to see itself differently than it has done in the past.

Getting Ready

This stage is where the Fish begins to dismantle their:

- Incorrect, diminishing or limiting values and beliefs.
- Discriminatory or privileged attitudes (whether superior or inferior).
- Behaviours that limit itself or others.

This phase also involves the Fish:

- Envisioning how they want to live their life authentically, congruently, and with integrity and taking action towards this.
- Learning and unlearning to gain understanding, skills, and tools to navigate and support themselves through the cycle.
- Changing how they value and interact with Fish that are "not like me".

Reaching Out

This stage of the cycle involves the Fish reaching out to other Fish to:

- Check its reality.
- Expose itself to a broader range of opinions, perspectives, and differences.

- Practice using new skills and tools.
- Experiment with expressing its views to other Fish.

The Fish may, at this stage find that others try to pressurise it into staying quiet, not making waves, and maintaining the status quo. Persistence is key here.

This phase moves the Fish from intrapersonal to interpersonal liberation.

Building Community

There are two steps to building community: communicating and interacting with:

- Fish that are "like me" for support. The Fish must have the same social identities and be committed to changing the system of oppression.
- Fish that are "not like me" to gain understanding and build coalitions. What is important here is that these Fish are not the "teachers".

In building a community, it is essential to talk about and minimise the barriers and boundaries that separate and divide the Fish. While these will not necessarily be eliminated (as the macrosystem still exists), their potency can be diminished. A conscious effort is required to navigate these areas continually.

Coalescing

It is here that the Fish join to form a powerful coalition and take action to tackle the system of oppression. It is here that Fish refuse to play their "socialised roles" and collude with the system. The Fish actively Ally, uniting and working together to make a difference and create change.

Creating Change

A commitment to creating permanent change shifts the entire culture of the Fishbowl and starts to detoxify the water. The Fish focus on the creation of new paradigms, roles, assumptions, and structures based on equality, equity, inclusion, and unity. By sharing power collectively, the Fish, the water, and the Fishbowl begin to transform and detoxify.

Maintaining

The past is not to be forgotten or ignored. History needs to be documented in an honest and inclusive way.

Healing will continue for a long time.

It is important to continue to nurture, strengthen, support, and integrate the changes so that trust continues to build and the changes become a permanent reality.

In this phase, the Fish remain peaceful, hopeful, and committed to sustaining the changes to ensure that the Fishbowl genuinely becomes equal, equitable, and inclusive.

Liberation is both personal and political – the Fish can be both the prisoner and the guard for their own sense of freedom.

Fish have the keys to free themselves.

Liberation is not about creating a new normal. Who wants normal? Normal does not celebrate or make space for individuality. It's time to say "fuck you" to normal and instead create a new reality where balance is restored and uniqueness is valued.

Fish can do better than normal.

IT'S TIME FOR ALL FISH TO

WAKE UP,

TAKE ACTION,

AND SWIM TOGETHER

"We need joy as we need air.
We need love as we need water.
We need each other as we need the earth
to share."

Maya Angelou

Lightning Source UK Ltd.
Milton Keynes UK
UKHW020130091020
371248UK00008B/80